Human Rights in Focus: Human Trafficking

Other titles in the *Human Rights in Focus* series include:

Human Rights in Focus: Human Trafficking

Leanne Currie-McGhee

San Diego, CA

© 2018 ReferencePoint Press, Inc.
Printed in the United States

For more information, contact:
ReferencePoint Press, Inc.
PO Box 27779
San Diego, CA 92198
www.ReferencePointPress.com

LIBRARY OF CONGRESS CATALOGING-IN-PUBLICATION DATA

Name: Currie-McGhee, Leanne, author.
Title: Human Rights in Focus: Human Trafficking/by Leanne Currie-McGhee.
Description: San Diego, CA: ReferencePoint Press, Inc., 2018. | Series:
  Human Rights in Focus | Includes bibliographical references and index. |
Audience: Grade 9 to 12.
Identifiers: LCCN 2017016050 (print)| ISBN 9781682822272 (hardback) |
ISBN 9781682822289 (eBook)
Subjects: LCSH: Human trafficking—United States—Juvenile literature. |
  Government policy—United States—Juvenile literature. | Human
  rights—United States—Juvenile literature

Contents

Modern-Day Slavery

"A significant number of people believe that slavery ended in 1863, when in fact, modern slavery exists in every corner of the globe,"[1] writes Somaly Mam, a survivor of sexual slavery. Sadly, Mam is correct. Today, millions of people are enslaved around the world, despite the fact that most governments officially abolished slavery more than one hundred years ago.

Modern-day slavery is also called human trafficking. This is when individuals are either forced or coerced into situations where they become the property of individual criminals or entire organizations. Traffickers use violence, threats, lies, and other manipulative tactics to force people to work for free or engage in the commercial sex trade. Victims must do whatever their traffickers demand, or suffer brutal consequences. Human trafficking often involves moving victims from one place to another, but this is not always the case. If a victim is forced to comply with a trafficker's bidding, the crime can be classified as human trafficking.

According to the International Labour Organization (ILO), human trafficking is a multibillion-dollar criminal industry that denies freedom to approximately 20.9 million men, women, and children around the world. Victims of human trafficking have virtually no control over their lives, and often go unrecognized as victims by those around them or broader society.

Never-Ending Debt

Traffickers often prey upon poor people. Consider the case of Haresh, of West Bengal, India, who wanted to marry a woman named Sarika. Because of local customs, he needed money to do so (in West Bengal, couples must pay several fees in order to officially marry). He therefore took a loan of $110 from a landowner who lived nearby and planned to pay it back by working for him for a couple months. However, the landowner kept increasing the amount Haresh owed him, and Haresh could not keep up. In a short amount of time, he had become what is known as a debt bonded laborer.

The landowner charged Haresh excessive amounts of money for daily needs such as food, repairs on his hut, and medical expenses. He also charged Haresh more than 100 percent interest on the amounts he owed each year. As a result Haresh and his family live in a never-ending cycle of debt and servitude. To pay off the constantly growing amount, Haresh and his family work fourteen or more hours a day, nearly every day of the year, with minimal food and water and no pay. Two decades after taking the initial loan, Haresh remains in servitude. "My entire family is still in debt to the landowner," he says. "Sarika and I work in the fields, my sons and their wives work at the brick kilns. One day

Prostitutes stand behind red-lit windows, on display for potential customers in Amsterdam's red light district. Amsterdam is a top destination for human trafficking where criminals force young women into the city's legal sex trade.

my grandchildren will work for the landowner. There is no way to repay these debts. We will only be free when we die."[2]

Haresh is just one of millions of bonded laborers in South Asia and elsewhere around the globe. Bonded laborers often enter into servitude with an initial loan, and are then exploited by their lenders. They need to take on more loans from different lenders to cover their various debts. As in Haresh's case, payments often vastly exceed the loan's worth. This is why once indebted, people are never able to pay off what they owe. Their families are brought into bondage, and the slavery continues.

Young and Lonely

Trafficking is not just a problem in poverty stricken areas. It takes place in nearly all countries, including wealthier ones like the United States. Lynne Marie Oddo learned this firsthand. Oddo lived in different foster homes throughout her childhood, separated from her parents and brothers, with no stable family. As a result, she grew up longing for close relationships and lacking confidence in herself. These vulnerabilities put her at grave risk to be taken advantage of by sex traffickers, who prey on people who have exactly these issues.

> "There is no way to repay these debts. We will only be free when we die."[2]
>
> —Haresh, victim of debt bondage

When Oddo was sixteen, two men named Joseph Defeis and Andy Fakhoury began taking her to parties, where they convinced her to try drugs. After many such parties, Defeis and Fakhoury persuaded Oddo to run away with them. Unhappy with her home life, she agreed. However, once they were away, the men raped her and forced her to have sex with others for money, which they pocketed. Oddo was scared to leave them. She worried that people would be angry with her for running away; she was also scared that Defeis and Fakhoury would hurt her if she left.

The men drugged Oddo to keep her under their control. They also kept her hidden inside their apartment. Oddo tried to escape several times, but it took three years before she was successful. At nineteen years old, she finally got away. Eventually, Oddo was able to testify against her traffickers, and they were ultimately convicted of sex trafficking and assault. Although she is now free,

Oddo continues to suffer repercussions from her horrific experience. "I get so sick to my stomach, I'm ready to curl up in a ball and cry, or scream and let it all out," she says. "At the same time, it doesn't come out. It doesn't come out."[3]

A Long, Hard Fight

By testifying against her traffickers, Oddo became part of ongoing efforts to combat human trafficking. Over the past two decades, many countries, particularly developed nations, have put a lot of time, effort, and resources into fighting this very serious human rights violation. They have raised awareness about how to report trafficking and help victims, have introduced legislation, and have increased law enforcement efforts to catch human traffickers and bring them to justice. Although there are multiple ongoing efforts to prosecute traffickers and provide assistance to victims, this is a very difficult problem to stop. Human trafficking has numerous causes, many of which are complex. In addition, because human trafficking often crosses borders and involves numerous countries—even multiple continents—it requires a lot of cooperation to address. Fighting this crime and bringing its perpetrators to justice will continue to be complex and challenging, but doing so is necessary to defend human rights.

Chapter 1

Understanding Human Trafficking

According to Polaris, an anti-human-trafficking organization, about 20.9 million people are currently enslaved worldwide. Almost every country in the world is affected by this issue, as either a place where victims originate from or as a destination where they end up—or both. Governments and law enforcement agencies have been working hard to shine a light on the dark world of human trafficking. Their primary goal is to rescue its victims and prosecute the perpetrators.

What Is Human Trafficking?

Human trafficking is slavery, and therefore a direct violation of people's basic human rights. Slavery is technically illegal in all countries, and is outlawed by the United Nations (UN). According to the UN's Universal Declaration of Human Rights, "No one shall be held in slavery or servitude; slavery and the slave trade shall be prohibited in all their forms."[4] Despite this, modern slavery such as human trafficking continues to take place. It occurs when individuals or organizations use threats, coercion, or violence to make people work as laborers against their will for little or no money, or perform sexual or other acts without their consent. Victims of human trafficking are in essence owned by other people, and as such are not allowed to make decisions about their work, movements, health, living conditions, relationships, and other essential aspects of life.

People often think that human trafficking means movement over city, state, or even country lines, but this is not necessarily true. Human trafficking can and often does feature the trade of people without any movement or boundary crossing.

It can be difficult to define human trafficking. The UN's 2003 Protocol to Prevent, Suppress, and Punish Trafficking in Persons, Especially Women and Children was the first global and legally binding instrument to put forth a definition on what trafficking in persons entails. It defines human trafficking as the recruitment, transportation, transfer, harboring, or receipt of people. It also defines human trafficking as using threat or force to control a victim with the purpose of exploiting him or her for profit or other benefits.

As of 2016, 187 countries had ratified the UN Protocol. By ratifying, they agreed to track, investigate, and fight human trafficking within their countries. In return the Protocol gives countries practical help in drafting laws and creating national anti-trafficking strategies, as well as offering resources for implementing them. The Protocol also helps countries develop approaches for establishing domestic criminal offenses for human trafficking and for prosecuting human trafficking cases. This is important, as human

The United Nations Headquarters building is shown in New York City. In 2003, the UN protocol was established as a global and binding agreement to investigate, track, and fight the spread of human trafficking.

trafficking is more effectively fought when countries are on the same page with their methods and procedures. According to Yury Fedotov, executive director of the United Nations Office on Drugs and Crime (UNODC), this is key for making progress. "We want to live in a world where human trafficking no longer exists," he says. "If we are to do this, we must unite and deliver effective and efficient action on the ground to achieve this goal. This means more cooperation, more political commitment, more determination to arrest, detain, and prosecute the guilty perpetrators."[5]

Types of Human Trafficking

The two most common types of human trafficking are sexual slavery and forced labor. Sexual slavery is when a person—typically a woman or child—is sexually exploited, either by being forced to engage in prostitution or being coerced into making pornography. According to the FBI, sexual slavery is the fastest-growing business of organized crime and the third-largest criminal enterprise in the world.

The other most common type of human trafficking is forced labor, which involves making people work under degrading conditions for either little or no pay. In all cases the victims are under force or threat to comply with the trafficker's demands. The main purpose of their exploitation is to earn the trafficker or trafficking ring money or other profits.

Although these two activities constitute the majority of human trafficking cases, there are other types, too. For example, perpetrators are increasingly trafficking in organs. In such cases, victims' organs are taken out of their bodies through coercion, force, or even unbeknownst to them. The organs are then sold to others, some of whom do not realize the organs were taken illegally. There is a growing market for trafficked organs because the demand for organ transplants is so high. According to the American Transplant Foundation, 123,000 people in the United States are on waiting lists to receive an organ, and a new name is added to the list every twelve minutes. On average, twenty-one people die each day due to the low availability of organs. As a result there is very strong demand for organs, in the United States and around the world.

Experts at the World Health Organization estimate that each year, ten thousand black market transactions involving human

Refugees Are Most Vulnerable

Desperate situations create opportunities for human trafficking. This is why refugees—people who live outside the borders of their countries—are at enormous risk for becoming trafficking victims.

The UN reports that there are about 21.3 million people registered as refugees, and more than half are under the age of eighteen. Refugee children are at particularly high risk for trafficking due to poverty and displacement. Without a home or income, refugees are more likely to accept debt bondage for themselves or their children as a way to bring in money or meet basic needs such as shelter and food.

Currently, Syrian refugee children are among those most at risk. According to UNICEF USA, "Crushing poverty and debt have forced Syrian refugee families to resort to desperate coping mechanisms that put children at a particularly high risk." Such coping mechanisms include allowing children to be used as laborers or be recruited by armed groups to work in militias. In fact, a recent survey by UNICEF USA found that nearly half of all Syrian refugee families living in Jordan are earning their money from the work of a child. Similarly, in Turkey, Syrian refugee girls as young as eight years old are engaging in child labor.

UNICEF USA, "If You Care About Trafficking, You Should Care About Refugees," January 25, 2016. www.unicefusa.org.

organs, many of which are obtained without the donors' permission, occur. The most frequently harvested organs are kidneys, as opposed to hearts or other body parts. This is because people can survive with just one kidney, so traffickers can usually get a person's kidney without killing them. A 2011 report by Global Financial Integrity estimates that the illegal organ trade generates between $600 million and $1.2 billion in profits per year.

Sadi Ahmed, of Pakistan, knows firsthand what it is like to be trafficked for organs. In 2016 a gang held Ahmed and twenty-four other people hostage for three months in an attempt to illegally harvest their kidneys. He and the other victims were lured to the city of Rawalpindi under the promise of getting a job, but this turned out to be a trick. Ahmed was taken to a building, locked inside of it, and his phone was confiscated. He was told to be quiet and not try to escape, or else he would be beaten.

Then the traffickers told Ahmed and the others that their kidneys would be tested to ensure they were healthy and to see if they matched the blood type and other needs of those who wanted to buy them. Ahmed was told he would be paid a small amount of money after his kidney was removed. "We were threatened that the police would beat us up and we would be killed,"[6] he says. Luckily, Ahmed was rescued just hours before he was scheduled to have his kidney removed at the nearby hospital. Others in Pakistan have not been so lucky, however: according to the Pakistan Transplantation Society, as many as one hundred illegal transplants take place in that country every month.

Child Soldiers

Another type of human trafficking involves forcing children to serve as soldiers. This crime is less publicized than other types of human trafficking because it does not affect as many victims around the world. However, in certain countries, particularly in those where there is internal conflict, thousands of children are affected. Due to a lack of access to these conflicts, it is difficult for organizations to accurately estimate how many children are forced to serve in armies. However, research by UNICEF (the United Nations Children's Fund) suggests there are tens of thousands of child soldiers around the world. For example, there are at least twelve thousand children currently used by armed forces and groups in South Sudan.

This crime occurs when rebel groups or government armies force, manipulate, blackmail, or otherwise coerce children into fighting for a military group's cause. This is especially a problem in countries where a high percentage of the population is young, and where there are ongoing civil wars or conflicts between multiple militias. In 2016 the US State Department identified ten countries whose governments, or militias supported by the government or active in the country, recruited and used children as soldiers in combat: Burma, the Democratic Republic of Congo, Iraq, Nigeria, Rwanda, Somalia, South Sudan, Sudan, Syria, and Yemen.

In 2014, during the height of the civil war in South Sudan, more than one hundred boys were kidnapped from their classrooms each day around the country and told they must fight in the war. Simon is a former child soldier in South Sudan who lost many years to combat. He was forced to serve for an armed group called Cobra Faction. His first duties included working for the group as a dishwasher and then a cook. During this time he did not attend school, he received little food, and he was beaten if he did not follow orders.

At just twelve years old, Simon was tasked with protecting a commander in the Cobra Faction. Armed with a gun, Simon spent his days guarding the commander as they made exhausting treks

A child soldier mans a checkpoint in the Democratic Republic of Congo. It is estimated that there are tens of thousands of child soldiers around the world, many of whom have been manipulated or forced to fight for a military group's cause.

through war zones, often placing Simon in the middle of the conflict. During his years in the Cobra Faction, he lived an arduous and violent life until he was finally released after a peace agreement was established between the government and Cobra Faction in 2014. Simon spent his first days of release at a UNICEF center, where he received medical care, clean water, food, and basic household items. He was finally reunited with his family in 2015. Today he attends school and attempts to return to a normal life.

Forced Marriage

Another type of human trafficking that disproportionally affects young people—particularly women—is forced marriage. This is when individuals are forced to enter into a marriage against their will and without their agreement. Unlike arranged marriages, where families set up meetings between individuals in the hopes they will agree to marry, forced marriages are not voluntary. As such, they are a direct violation of the UN's Universal Declaration of Human Rights, which states that a woman's right to choose a spouse and enter freely into marriage is central to her life, dignity, and equality as a human being. The UN Population Fund (UNFPA) estimates that between 2011 and 2020, more than 140 million girls will be forced to marry. "Child marriage is an appalling violation of human rights and robs girls of their education, health and long-term prospects,"[7] says Dr. Babatunde Osotimehin, the UNFPA executive director.

> "Child marriage is an appalling violation of human rights and robs girls of their education, health and long-term prospects."[7]
>
> —Dr. Babatunde Osotimehin, executive director, United Nations Population Fund

Lana, a university student, was forced into marriage after being tricked, drugged, and kidnapped from her home in Vietnam. Lana's nightmare began when she met up with a friend she had made online. After a few drinks, she felt tired and wanted to go home; pretty soon, she fell asleep. The next day, she found herself in a car with several other girls being smuggled across the border into China.

Kidnapping and forced marriage is a risk for girls like Lana, who live in the villages along the Vietnamese-Chinese border. Many are trafficked into China, where a shortage of women has created a demand for brides—even illegal, bonded ones. Vietnamese teenage girls are tricked or drugged, smuggled across the border, and then sold for as little as $3,000 to the end buyer. At all points in the process they are seen not as humans, but as commodities or products.

Lana was forced into a marriage that took years to escape. Eventually, Chinese police helped her return to Vietnam, but she had to leave behind a baby she had produced as a result of the marriage.

Countries and Trends

One reason Lana was vulnerable to human trafficking is that Vietnam's government does not fully meet the minimum standards for eliminating trafficking that have been set by the Trafficking Victim's Protection Act, a law passed by the US Congress. As such, Vietnam is rated a Tier 2 country according to the US State Department's 2016 *Trafficking in Persons* report. This report divides countries into four tiers—1, 2, 2 watch list, and 3—based on the country's efforts to combat human trafficking. The lowest level, Tier 1, means a country meets the standards for combating human trafficking through prosecutions and convictions. Tier 2 means a country is not meeting minimum standards, but is making significant efforts to do so, while Tier 2 watch list means that while the country is making efforts, its number of victims is significantly increasing. Tier 3 countries, meanwhile, do not meet minimum standards and are not making any significant effort to do so. Vietnam is a Tier 2 because, for example, while the Vietnamese government provided anti-trafficking training for officials in 2015, many still lacked the skills to identify victims or to investigate labor trafficking cases.

While people who live in higher tier countries are more at risk for becoming victims of human trafficking, even Tier 1 countries face considerable challenges in fighting the problem. For example, although the United States is a Tier 1 country, human trafficking is a considerable problem there, and reports of human trafficking increase each year. Polaris reported that in the United States, 8,042 cases of human trafficking were reported to them in 2016, which was a 35 percent increase from 2015.

The US State Department's tiers are one tool that those who fight human trafficking rely on to assess the scope of the problem.

Another such tool involves studies that aim to pinpoint the movement and flow of human trafficking victims. The UN has found that most victims are transported from poorer regions to more affluent ones. Trafficking also often includes bringing victims across country lines. In fact, as stated in the 2016 *Global Report on Trafficking in Persons* by the UNODC, from 2012 to 2014, 57 percent of known victims were moved across at least one international border. The key destination areas for transregional human trafficking (the name for cross-border cases) are Western and Southern Europe, wealthier countries in the Middle East (such as Kuwait and Qatar), and North America (primarily the United States). The major points of origin for human trafficking victims—that is, where most victims come from—include countries in South Asia (such as Nepal), East Asia (such as Vietnam), and sub-Saharan Africa, including Sudan and the Congo. Some countries, such as Russia, Thailand, and South Africa, are origin and destination points. However, most countries tend to be one or the other.

Awareness Makes a Difference

A key part of fighting human trafficking involves helping the public to identify and report this crime. In 2011, Sheila Frederick, an Alaska Airlines flight attendant, was able to do just that. Frederick was working a flight from Seattle to San Francisco and noticed a teenage passenger who had greasy blond hair. Frederick noticed the girl was traveling with an older, well-dressed man, which made her suspicious. When Frederick tried to speak with the pair, the man became defensive.

Frederick felt uneasy about the situation. Under her breath, she told the girl to go to the bathroom, where she had stuck a note to the mirror. Frederick left a message for the girl, and a pen so they could communicate. "She wrote back on the note that she needed help," said Frederick. Upon reading the note, Frederick notified the pilot and when the plane landed at the terminal, police were waiting.

Since then, Frederick has spoken at a training workshop organized by the nonprofit organization Airline Ambassadors. She and others teach flight attendants to look for passengers who appear frightened, ashamed, or nervous, or who are children traveling with an adult who does not appear to be a parent or a relative.

Quoted in Fox 8, "Flight Attendant Saves Teen from Human Trafficking," February 6, 2017. http://myfox8.com.

Even in cases of domestic human trafficking (where victims are moved within one country), victims tend to be transported from poorer areas to wealthier ones and from rural zones to cities, tourist centers, or industrial areas. The reason why traffickers often transport victims to wealthier areas is because their ultimate goal is to profit from them—as such, they need wealthy clients who can pay. Indeed, human trafficking is highly profitable. In 2014 the ILO estimated that $150 billion is generated each year from this criminal activity. Of these profits, two-thirds result from sexual exploitation, while another $51 billion results from forced labor exploitation, including housekeepers and servants, agriculture, and other activities.

Who Are the Traffickers?

Traffickers may work alone or as part of a larger ring. Generally, traffickers are from the same area as their victims. This makes it easier for them to connect with a victim via a common link. According to the *Global Report on Trafficking in Persons,* "This link may be family or affective ties, a shared gender, a common citizenship, the same hometown or village, a common language, culture or ethnic group, or a combination of these."[8]

Traffickers are also predominantly male. However, women are increasingly working as traffickers. While it is impossible to know how many traffickers exist and what their gender is, the UNODC can make estimates based on who is arrested and convicted of this crime. According to the UNODC, as of 2016 nearly 40 percent of convictions for human trafficking involved women. In some cases these women are former victims who became part of the criminal organization that exploited them. In other cases, however, it is women who actually lead the organization. The *Global Report on Trafficking in Persons* noted that in Azerbaijan, for example, two sisters were convicted of organizing a criminal network that trafficked at least nine women into other countries.

Who Are the Victims?

The victims of human trafficking are overwhelmingly women and children; they make up 79 percent of all victims. However, the UN

Runaway and homeless youth can be desperate to escape their harsh surroundings, making them prime targets of human traffickers.

has found that an increasing number of men are also being targeted, particularly as victims are increasingly trafficked for forced labor. The 2016 UNODC report detailed that the percentage of men trafficked grew from 13 percent in 2004 to 21 percent in 2014. There is a link between region and a victim's gender and age. For example, according to the UN, in eastern Europe and Central Asia, men made up more than 50 percent of those who are trafficked. In sub-Saharan Africa, however, children make up the majority of those who are trafficked, while men represent a relatively small share of the victims. The age and gender distribution of a country's population, in addition to the type of trafficking, further influences who becomes a victim.

People most vulnerable to exploitation are those who endure war, homelessness, poverty, and natural disasters. These crises make individuals more likely to lack basic necessities, need basic resources, and have few options for help, which renders them prone to coercion and force. Above all, these situations create people who are desperate to escape their current surroundings or reality, which makes them ripe for exploitation. "While human trafficking spans all demographics, there are some circumstances or vulnerabilities that lead to a higher susceptibility to victimization and human trafficking," notes Polaris. "Runaway and homeless youth, as well as victims of domestic violence, sexual assault, war or conflict, or social discrimination are frequently targeted by traffickers."[9]

No matter what circumstances lead a person to become a victim of human trafficking, the result is that his or her basic human rights are violated. Victims must cope with physical and emotional violations that have long-lasting, detrimental effects. International efforts are focusing more light on this crime, with numerous successes and triumphs. But with over an estimated 20 million people still enslaved throughout the world, the fight against human trafficking is just beginning.

> "Runaway and homeless youth, as well as victims of domestic violence, sexual assault, war or conflict, or social discrimination are frequently targeted by traffickers."[9]
>
> —Polaris, a nonprofit anti-trafficking organization

Chapter 2

Sex Trafficking

Focus Questions

1. What are some reasons why sex trafficking victims may be reluctant to contact authorities about their situation, if the opportunity to do so arose?
2. Why do you think runaways and foster children are especially vulnerable to sex trafficking?
3. How might awareness programs change the way people view victims of sex trafficking?

Karla Jacinto, of Mexico City, was just twelve years old when a twenty-two-year-old man lured her away from her home life. Jacinto was easy prey; she had been abused as a child and felt unloved and mistreated by her mother. As a result she soaked up the man's kind words to her and accepted rides in his fast, sleek car. Within a week of meeting, the man convinced Jacinto to run away with him. For their first three months together, he bought her chocolates and clothes, and gave her lots of attention. Then everything changed. The man told her that in order to stay with him, she must start having sex with other men, charge money for it, and give all the money to him—otherwise, he would kick her out.

Jacinto did not know what to do and had nowhere else to go. So she stayed with her trafficker, who soon moved her to the city of Guadalajara, where she was forced to sexually service at least twenty customers a day, seven days a week. "I started at 10 a.m. and finished at midnight," says Jacinto. "Some men would laugh at me because I was crying. I had to close my eyes so that I wouldn't see what they were doing to me, so that I wouldn't feel anything."[10] This horror continued for four years. Jacinto was sent to brothels, roadside motels, and even individual homes. Just when Jacinto did not think her situation could get worse, at age fifteen she discovered she was pregnant. She gave birth to a child who was immediately taken away from her.

When she was sixteen years old, police rescued Jacinto during an anti-trafficking raid. However, the scars of that life remain with her, and her attempt to recover emotionally and physically has been difficult.

> "I had to close my eyes so that I wouldn't see what they were doing to me, so that I wouldn't feel anything."[10]
>
> —Karla Jacinto, sex trafficking victim

Types of Sex Trafficking

Jacinto is one of millions of women around the world who have been victimized by sex trafficking, which is the most common human trafficking crime—it makes up 79 percent of all such trafficking offenses. Women and children are sex traffickers' main targets. These victims are exploited for the purposes of prostitution, pornography, and strip club work. Traffickers may use their victims for one or all of these types of sex trafficking, depending on how much money they can make.

Prostitution is the main industry in which sex trafficked victims are forced to work. This is in part because it is one of the most profitable illegal industries, and traffickers have the potential to make considerable sums of money through their victims' work. During prostitution, victims are forced to perform sexual acts for those who pay. Victims typically receive little or no portion of the money, and engage in the acts because their traffickers force them to, not because they choose to. While not all prostitutes are victims of sex trafficking, in the United States, all prostitutes under age eighteen are considered victims, as they are not legally adults who are able to give consent or permission to engage in sexual acts.

Another focus of sex trafficking is pornography, in which photos or movies are taken of people either naked or engaging in sexual acts. Sex traffickers often sell such movies and photos online. Globally, pornography is a $97-billion industry, according to Kassia Wosick, assistant professor of sociology at New Mexico

Pornography is estimated to be a $97-billion industry. Sex traffickers will often force their victims into making pornography.

State University, and between $10 billion and $12 billion comes from customers in the United States.

Traffickers may also use sexually explicit photos to force certain women or girls to become prostitutes, or keep them working as such. Indeed, traffickers often blackmail their victims by threatening to make photos of them public or send them to their families. "It is possible for a young woman or girl to walk away from sex trafficking and start a new life, but sexually illicit photos or films will follow her forever—regardless of whether she was underage when they were taken or not," explains Michelle Lille, who works for Human Trafficking Search, an organization that provides data and information about human trafficking. "Once a film or image with the girl's face is uploaded onto the Internet, it is there forever. Traffickers know this and use it as a method of control and blackmail, letting the girls know that now they are on the Internet they can never escape the life."[11]

Sex traffickers also force their victims to work in strip clubs. Here, women are recruited to work as hostesses, servers, or dancers. They are required to work or dance in various states of undress and engage in sex acts with customers. These victims are forced to follow schedules set by their traffickers and are frequently moved between multiple clubs, as traffickers try to avoid being caught.

The Victims

Women make up the vast majority of the estimated 1.35 million people forced to serve in the sex trade industry each year. According to the ILO, women account for 98 percent of victims. Many of these victims are very young. Children make up 40 percent to 50 percent of those forced to work in the sex industry.

Several circumstances can make a person vulnerable to becoming a victim of sex trafficking. These include being socially isolated, being addicted to drugs, experiencing violence at home, having a history of child sexual abuse, experiencing severe family dysfunction, failing out of school, or having a history of criminal behavior. People who experience any of these problems are more prone to being taken advantage of by a trafficker.

Young people are particularly at risk if their childhood has been marked by emotional trauma or abandonment, and they crave emotional support; this typically makes it easier for a trafficker to gain a victim's trust. In fact, according to the National Center for Missing & Exploited Children, 86 percent of runaway children in the United States who were forced into sex work came from the child welfare system, from foster homes or group homes. Traffickers exploit these children's emotional needs. They offer them kind words, give them gifts, and pretend to love and befriend them so as to persuade the youths to work for them. K.A., who is serving a life sentence for prostituting a fifteen-year-old, explains, "If you meet a female, she don't got no family, she don't got nowhere to stay, but you got a little bit of money, you doing for her, you putting a roof over her head, feeding her . . . she going to end up trusting you, depending on you."[12] Other traffickers use similar methods to gain their victims' trust and lure them into service.

The Traffickers

Most sex traffickers are typically people who have certain things in common with their victims, such as speaking the same language, originating from the same town or city, or sharing a cultural background. Having commonalities allows traffickers to better understand their victims, which helps them exploit their vulnerabilities. For example, if a sex trafficker is from the same neighborhood as the victim, and understands it is a poor area with little opportunities, he or she can initially befriend the victim and promise a better, wealthier life.

A prostitute leans in to talk to a potential customer in a car. Sex trafficking is very profitable because the victims can be exploited over and over again for years.

Traffickers might work alone. They may also be part of a small group or a member of a large criminal organization. What all traffickers share is the motivation to sexually exploit victims in order to make a profit. In industrialized nations, each sexually trafficked victim can earn up to $67,000 per year for a trafficker, according to the ILO. Recruiters—whose job is to initially lure victims into a trafficking system—can make an estimated $5,000 per victim pulled into service.

One reason sex trafficking is so profitable is because victims can be exploited again and again, like machines. Unlike the profits earned from selling drugs—which are consumed just once and then need to be replenished—sex trafficking victims can earn profits for their traffickers over and over again, and over many years. In addition, trafficking is lucrative because of the large numbers of people willing to pay for sex acts. The fact that sex trafficking is such a profitable industry drives traffickers to find victims to exploit.

> "If you meet a female, she don't got no family, she don't got nowhere to stay, but you got a little bit of money, you doing for her … she going to end up trusting you, depending on you."[12]
>
> —K.A., sex trafficker

Trafficker Methods

Depending on how they obtain their victims, sex traffickers are either known as "guerilla pimps" or "Romeo pimps." Guerilla pimps use physical violence, force, and abduction to victimize young women and girls; they often kidnap their victims into service. Romeo pimps, on the other hand, are the more common kind of trafficker. They get their victims to join them by preying on their vulnerabilities, which might include being extremely poor or living with an abusive parent. During the recruitment phase, victims are generally promised a better life, the opportunity to go to school, job skills training, a viable or good job, marriage, and care. The FBI suggests that traffickers tend to promise their victims a lifestyle they do not otherwise have access to. Traffickers may also claim to love and need their victims, making them feel an emotional obligation. Another way to obtain victims is to buy them from parents, husbands, and significant others; this is more likely to happen in the world's poorer

Super Bowl Sex Trafficking

Major tourist events often lead to spikes in sex trafficking. As a result, law enforcement officials in cities that host events like the Super Bowl are increasingly on alert for this potential problem. The Super Bowl often brings over a hundred thousand people to town, some of whom are looking to pay for sexual acts. Sex traffickers use this as an opportunity to gain more business. Nita Belles, director of the anti-trafficking group In Our Backyard, says, "When you have a male-dominated kind of attendance, then you will have additional trafficking coming in."

To prevent these illegal transactions, host cities are increasingly running sex trafficking awareness campaigns prior to the Super Bowl. Local law enforcement agencies are finding that some of their efforts to crack down on sex trafficking and exploitation are meeting with success. For example, during the 2017 Super Bowl in Houston, 183 potential buyers and 9 sex traffickers were arrested.

Quoted in Steven Romo, "Advocacy Groups Working to Stop Sex Trafficking During Super Bowl Weekend," ABC13, February 2, 2017. http://abc13.com.

regions. Once the victims are in their company, traffickers typically take their forms of identity—including birth certificates, passports, and drivers' licenses—to reduce their ability to escape.

Once recruited, victims are often locked in rooms or brothels for weeks or months. During this time they are drugged, terrorized, beaten, and raped. "These continual abuses make it easier for the traffickers to control their victims," write Amanda Walker-Rodriguez and Rodney Hill, who work on the Maryland Human Trafficking Task Force. "The captives are so afraid and intimidated that they rarely speak out against their traffickers, even when faced with an opportunity to escape."[13] As a result of the abuse and horrific treatment, some victims develop Stockholm syndrome. This is a condition in which individuals feel attached to their captors because of their complete dependence on them. Stockholm syndrome makes it less likely that victims will try to get away or report the crime to authorities.

Sex Trafficking Hotspots

Where a person lives impacts her chance of becoming a sex trafficking victim. While sex trafficking occurs across the globe, certain regions are more likely to produce victims. Victims are often taken from South and Southeast Asia, Central Asia, Central and South America, and other less developed areas. They are moved to more developed areas in Asia, the Middle East, Western Europe, and North America, where there are people willing to pay high prices for sexual acts. Although there are exceptions, victims are generally moved from poor countries and trafficked into relatively wealthier ones. In this way, sex trafficking is truly an international problem.

Trafficking usually occurs intra-regionally, with the highest number of sex trafficking victims moved between countries within regions, particularly in Asia. For example, the trafficking of girls from Nepal to India for forced prostitution is one of the busiest slave trafficking routes in the world. UNICEF estimates that seven thousand Nepali women and girls are trafficked into India each year.

Women rescued from brothels in India are lined up at a shelter in Nepal to identify an alleged trafficker. The trafficking of girls from Nepal to India for prostitution is one of the busiest trafficking routes in the world.

Sunita Dunawar was one of these girls. At age fourteen, her parents sold her to two men who took her to Mumbai, India, where she was forced to sexually service up to thirty clients a day. "If you don't do this work, I'll cut you up and throw you on the street like a stray dog,"[14] Dunawar recalls a man with a knife saying to her once. If she refused clients' requests, the men would burn her with cigarettes. A police raid freed Dunawar at age sixteen, and she eventually returned home to help prevent other girls from becoming trafficking victims.

In the United States, sex trafficking is most prevalent in California, Texas, Florida, Ohio, and New York, according to the National Human Trafficking Hotline. Tourist areas and places that have a large transient population usually experience higher levels of sex trafficking. The city of Miami is one such place. "We have a booming tourism industry," says Wifredo Ferrer, US attorney for

Cybersex Dens

Technology has increased sex traffickers' abilities to exploit their victims. An example of how comes from Andrea, a fourteen-year-old girl who was lured away from her village in the Philippines by a cousin who told her he would give her a well-paying job as a babysitter in the city. Instead, Andrea was placed in a home with other girls and was not allowed to leave.

The windows of the house were covered, the rooms were darkened, and a computer and camera were set up for filming. Then Andrea and the others girls were forced to perform sexual acts while being filmed and watched online by buyers. Customers paid $56 per minute, typed instructions into their computer, and then watched, via a live camera, as the girls performed the acts. "I was told if I tried to escape, the police would put me in jail," says Andrea.

After three months one of the girls escaped, told the authorities, and Andrea and the other girls were rescued. She served as a witness in a case against her abusers, but has received death threats. "I want them to be punished but I have moved far away to Manila because I am scared for my life," she says.

Quoted in Sunshine de Leon, "Cyber-Sex Trafficking: A 21st Century Scourge," CNN, July 17, 2013. www.cnn.com.

the Southern District of Florida. "We have a very active transient male population here, where guys come and go. If they are here for sporting events, for example, a lot of these victims are used, so to speak, to service them."[15]

Documenting Sex Trafficking

Fighting and preventing sex trafficking requires officials to obtain accurate information on the problem, such as how many traffickers there are, how many victims are involved, and where trafficking is occurring. This is the best way for authorities to determine how to pursue and prosecute traffickers and rescue victims. However, many countries have trouble collecting accurate and reliable data. As a result the numbers may underrepresent the actual extent of the problem.

One impediment to collecting data is that many countries lack the capacity and resources to properly track sex trafficking. Poorer countries particularly do not have enough money to extensively monitor the problem. Because poorer countries are also where victims are more likely to come from, there is probably a significant underrepresentation of global victims.

Another obstacle to obtaining data is that victims are often unwilling or unable to report abuse to officials. In parts of Asia, such as Vietnam, Burma, and Nepal, many people shame female victims for engaging in any sexual act outside of marriage, whether it was consensual or forced. Because of this aspect of the culture, sex trafficking victims might feel too humiliated to report their traffickers. Victims may also be prosecuted for committing a crime like prostitution, even if they were coerced into it. Still others fear that no one will be able to help. "I was really scared about who to tell," says Emily Sims, a survivor of sex trafficking. "There weren't a lot of public awareness campaigns about resources for sexual assault survivors, and I was ashamed to tell my family."[16] Sims now runs the Marin County Human Trafficking Task Force, a nonprofit agency based in Northern California.

> "There weren't a lot of public awareness campaigns about resources for sexual assault survivors, and I was ashamed to tell my family."[16]
>
> —Emily Sims, sex trafficking victim

Predicted Increase in Trafficking

To help victims like Sims, more countries are raising awareness of this critical problem by launching campaigns to encourage citizens to report sex trafficking should they see or suspect it. As the problem is more frequently and more reliably reported, there will likely be more and higher quality data about it.

On the other hand, many experts predict that sex trafficking is likely to grow. This is because the high demand will continue and the potential to profit is great. "The overwhelming numbers of desperate people and the profitability of sex slaves likely means that even if we cannot yet accurately pinpoint the growth in the global population of sex slaves, it is likely to get worse before it gets better,"[17] writes Heather M. Smith, assistant professor of international affairs at Lewis & Clark College. To combat this growth, it is critical to promote awareness, action, and prosecution. For its part, the US Department of Defense has increased training for its employees about all forms of trafficking, including sex trafficking. It is equally important to teach citizens and others to recognize the signs of sex trafficking and how to report it, and help victims realize their acts are only shameful for the traffickers and buyers. Lifting the veil on sex trafficking can save the lives of millions of young women and girls.

Chapter 3

Forced Labor

Focus Questions

1. Why do you think poverty or sudden financial strife might lead a person to become a victim of forced labor?
2. Should parents who allow their children to become victims of human trafficking be prosecuted? Why or why not?
3. Do you think a forced laborer who is illegally smuggled across country lines should be allowed to stay in the country? Why or why not?

Flor Molina was the mother of three young children in Mexico when she decided to take sewing classes. She hoped to learn skills that would help her find a good job so as to better herself and her family. Her sewing teacher told Molina that if she moved to the United States, she could make a lot of money as a seamstress. The teacher persuaded Molina to leave her home, her children, and her mother for an opportunity the teacher arranged. Molina thought it was a good idea; she believed she would be able to make enough money to send some home every month.

The day she arrived in Los Angeles, however, Molina realized she had made a grave mistake. "I quickly realized it had all been a lie," she says. "My trafficker told me that now I owe her almost $3,000 for bringing me to the U.S. and that I had to work for her in order to pay her back."[18] Molina was forced to work eighteen hours a day sewing dresses that the traffickers sold for $200 in department stores. She then had to stay after her shift to clean the factory. Her trafficker forced her to sleep in the storage room, where she shared a single mattress with another victim. She was allowed to eat only one meal a day. Molina had become a forced laborer.

After a few weeks, a coworker—who was a legitimate worker—thought that something about Molina's circumstances seemed odd. For one, she noticed Molina never went home after work. She quietly slipped Molina a piece of paper that had her phone number on it and a note that said to call if she needed help. After several weeks Molina persuaded her trafficker to allow her to go to church. Once outside, she found a pay phone. After finding someone who spoke Spanish who could explain to her how to use the phone, she called the coworker, who helped her contact the authorities, and eventually the FBI. The FBI connected Molina with the Coalition to Abolish Slavery and Trafficking (CAST), a nonprofit group that helped her regain her life.

A Profitable, Illicit Business

Molina's story is not unusual. Around the world, according to the ILO, approximately three out of one thousand people are trapped in jobs they were either forced or coerced into, and from which they cannot escape. As with sex trafficking, the main motivation for engaging in forced laborer trafficking is the high profits it can yield. The ILO estimates that forced laborers generate approximately $51 billion in profits a year for traffickers. Broken down per individual, a trafficker can make about $4,800 per year per forced labor factory worker, $2,500 per agriculture laborer, and $2,300 per forced domestic worker. Because human labor is reusable, traffickers are able to profit off their victims year after year.

Industries risk using forced laborers when they want to significantly reduce their costs and increase their profits. For example, according to a Tulane University survey of child labor from 2013 to 2014, producers of cacao (the raw ingredient of chocolate) in the Ivory Coast and Ghana—two regions that account for roughly 60 percent to 70 percent of the global cacao supply—have used more than 2.3 million children to work in cacao production. By forcing children to work, and paying them either nothing or very little, plantation owners are able to keep more of the money they make from selling the cacao.

Bonded Labor

Bonded labor is the most common form of forced labor. In bonded labor, a person agrees to work to repay a loan, or to pay a fee for

In the Ivory Coast a worker collects cacao beans after they have dried in the sun. The Ivory Coast and Ghana have used more than 2.3 million children to work in cacao production.

being escorted across a border. However, what a bonded laborer quickly discovers is that he or she has been tricked into working for little to no pay, with no chance of repaying the debt. This is because the debt constantly grows and changes to unobtainable amounts. As a result the victim is kept in bondage indefinitely.

People become bonded laborers due to insurmountable poverty or sudden financial setback. This is often the case in South Asia, an area with many poor regions. According to the Anti-Slavery Organization, a nonprofit group that combats human trafficking, bonded labor flourishes in South Asia's agricultural industries, brick kilns, mills, mines, and factories. For example, in India, hundreds of thousands of men, women, and children suffer extreme exploitation and abuse as forced laborers.

One of these laborers is a woman named Puspal. She and her husband became workers in an Indian brick kiln to support their family, but soon found that they made almost no money. The kiln owner would not allow them to stop working, telling them they owed a debt for the basic shelter and food they received while working. Forced labor had a brutal effect on Puspal's entire family. "My family had been working in a kiln for five years but didn't seem to be earning any money. Whenever we asked, the debt was still not paid," Puspal explains. "On a promise of a commission we brought more families from Chhattisgarh [a state in India], but the new workers were not paid and were starving. They tried to leave, but two got caught and they locked them up and beat them."[19]

Puspal and her family finally escaped their situation with the help of the organization Volunteers for Social Justice, which helped them find temporary housing. However, Puspal's family is still poor, and she worries about how they will survive in the future.

Private Economy Slavery

Puspal's forced labor was an example of labor by private economy slavery, where people and companies are the traffickers. Private economy slavery is the most prominent form of forced labor, accounting for 90 percent of all such offenses. It is prevalent in industries that feature low-income workforces that are more vulnerable to exploitation. These include agriculture, construction, manufacturing, hospitality, landscaping, building maintenance, textile production, domestic work, and mining. The ILO estimates that female forced laborers are most commonly placed in domestic work, while men and boys primarily work in agriculture, construction, and mining.

A specific type of private economy slavery is known as involuntary domestic servitude. This is when a victim is forced to work in a private residence. Involuntary domestic workers perform household duties similar to maids, housekeepers, nannies, and assistants. However, they are not free to leave their employment, are often abused, and are underpaid, if paid at all. They work long hours without days off, and under grueling conditions. Such situations are difficult to track and disrupt, since victims are isolated in someone's private home. Domestic servitude can also be difficult to detect because traffickers use many tactics to prevent victims from escaping or reporting the crime. For example, they may bring victims in from another country and then confiscate their passports.

Bidemi Bello, a Nigerian-born US citizen living in Georgia, forced two Nigerian women into domestic slavery for four years. Bello used her connections in Nigeria to recruit two women to come work for her in the United States. She told them they would be paid and have an opportunity to go to school. Once they were brought to Georgia, however, the women were physically abused, given spoiled food to eat, isolated, and made to work long hours doing housework and providing childcare for no pay. Bello was convicted of trafficking after the women escaped and testified against her. "The evidence showed that this was a case of modern-day slavery

Natural Disasters and Human Trafficking

Natural disasters can create an environment that makes individuals and families vulnerable to human trafficking. This is what happened in April 2015, when a massive earthquake hit Nepal and left millions of people struggling to survive. One of them is Prem Tamang, who lost his home and farm. His family was forced to move from their village to find work elsewhere.

Human traffickers target families like Tamang's. With few other options, many desperate people struggling to survive in the wake of a natural disaster are attracted to human traffickers' promises of decent-paying overseas work or educational opportunities for children. Many natural disaster survivors succumb and become housecleaners in the Middle East, providers of slave labor in South Asia, or mining workers in South America.

Nepalese police and activists estimate that forced labor has increased 15 percent to 20 percent since the earthquake. The Tamang family has lived under corrugated tin shelters, and has survived two rainy monsoon seasons by eating rice provided by emergency relief organizations. Despite these difficulties, Tamang and his family have thus far resisted human trafficking. Tamang currently works independently for $2 a day, clearing rubble from someone else's home. However, Tamang worries about how long they can survive. "We don't even have a place to sleep. We're just sleeping outside," he says. For now, he and his family are getting by without agreeing to a deal from a trafficker—but just barely.

Quoted in Stephen Groves, "Nepal Earthquake Survivors Are Falling Prey to Human Trafficking," PRI, November 15, 2016. www.pri.org.

hidden within an expensive home in an upscale neighborhood,"[20] says Sally Quillian Yates, US attorney for the Northern District of Georgia.

Countries of Concern

Although thousands of forced laborers exist in the United States and other wealthy countries, the Asia-Pacific region is home to the greatest portion of forced laborers, with more than half the total number of forced workers worldwide. According to the ILO, this region enslaves approximately 11.7 million people. Africa has the second highest number of forced laborers (an estimated 3.7 million), and is followed by Latin America and the Caribbean (1.8 million).

One reason these regions are hotspots for forced labor is that in some places, the practice is culturally tolerated, even if it is officially against the law. This is the case in Africa, which has an estimated four forced laborers per one thousand inhabitants. "Ongoing conflicts, extremes of poverty, high levels of corruption and the impact of resource exploitation to feed global markets all increase the risk of enslavement in many African countries,"[21] reports the Global Slavery Index. For example, in Mauritania, the practice is made worse by the fact that the thousands of adults and children who are forced laborers are illiterate and unaware of their rights. They are "owned" by cattle herders, who might even sell them to other slave owners. The victims are taught that they are slaves because it is the will of God. Without access to education or legal help, they continue to be victimized.

In other countries, governments may not perceive some acts as forced labor, even though the UN has categorized the activities as such. For instance, in Middle Eastern countries like Qatar, regulations exist that actually make it legal for employers to exploit migrant labor, even though it violates workers' rights. For example, under the provisions of Qatar's sponsorship law—which says that a migrant worker must be sponsored

> "Ongoing conflicts, extremes of poverty, high levels of corruption and the impact of resource exploitation to feed global markets all increase the risk of enslavement in many African countries."[21]
>
> —Global Slavery Index, which estimates slavery operations around the world

by his or her employer in order to enter the country—sponsors have the unilateral power to cancel workers' residency permits, deny workers the ability to change employers, and deny workers permission to leave the country. This power allows employers to exploit their migrant workers.

In other countries, governments not only overlook but also actively participate in the forced labor industry. Consider the case of Uzbekistan, which is the world's fifth-largest cotton-exporting nation. When it is time to harvest the cotton, the government drafts about a million people, most of whom are employees in the public

A woman picks cotton in Uzbekistan, the fifth-largest cotton-exporting nation. At harvest time the government drafts about 1 million people, who receive little to no pay and can be arrested if they refuse to work.

sector or work as professionals, to pick it. "You come to work, with all the makeup, wearing nice clothes, good shoes," explains Tamara Khidoyatova, a sixty-one-year-old doctor, of her experience, "and the polyclinic director runs in and says, 'I need 40 people in the field, the bus is outside, hurry, hurry!'"[22] Sometimes the workers must pick cotton for a day; other times, they must work for weeks. Pickers carry heavy cloth sacks around their necks, and they pick until they collect the quota of 120 pounds of raw cotton a day. For their work, they receive little to no pay. At night, they sleep on cots in the gymnasiums of village schools or in barracks in the fields, until the required amount of cotton is collected. If citizens defy the government and refuse to work in the fields, they may be arrested and jailed.

Who Is Vulnerable?

Economics and country conflicts significantly factor into whether a person is vulnerable to becoming a victim of forced labor. Poverty is a major risk factor: People desperate to support themselves and their families are often enslaved. Traffickers know this and prey on those in poverty. They promise decent pay and good jobs if the person accepts work with them. An ILO study in Pakistan found that in the lower Sindh Province, an area marked by significant poverty, 66 percent of residents worked as bonded laborers.

Regional conflicts also cause specific segments of populations to become victims of human trafficking. Armed conflicts in Southeast and Central Asia, Africa, Europe, and Latin America have caused millions of people to leave or be forced from their homes. These displaced people and refugees are often homeless, poor, and lack property; as a result, they are very vulnerable to exploitative forces. To survive, families are forced to rely on risky propositions that include allowing themselves or their children to be trafficked in exchange for some income, shelter, or food. Adding to the problem is that governments in areas of conflict are less equipped to address trafficking; many lack the resources to enforce anti-trafficking laws and prosecute traffickers.

Refugee populations in certain parts of the world are increasing, which adds to the human trafficking problem. Since early 2015 the number of refugees traveling to Europe from Africa and the Middle East has significantly increased, and many of them

How Fish Depletion Contributes to Slavery

The United States imported more than $34 billion in seafood products in 2015 largely from suppliers in China, Thailand, Vietnam, Indonesia, Canada, and Ecuador. As a result, fish populations in some countries have become depleted, forcing fishers to travel farther afield to catch fish. These longer trips raise fuel and labor costs, which has led some fishing companies to turn to forced labor to save money. Forced labor is particularly easy to hide at sea, where there are few authorities or even other people.

This is what happened to Lang Long of Cambodia, who accepted what he thought was an offer to travel to Thailand for a construction job. But once he arrived, Long was placed in a room that was guarded by armed men, near the port at Samut Prakan, Thailand. Then he and six others were herded up a gangway onto a rickety wooden fishing boat, where he would spend three brutal years in captivity. His time was spent trawling for forage fish, which are small and cheaply priced. Long was sold to two other fishing boats over the years, and he was shackled around the neck after he tried to escape. Eventually, Long's misery ended when an aid group discovered him and freed him.

have relied on human smugglers to help them cross international borders illegally. Some smugglers have forced them into servitude as repayment. Other refugees, upon arrival, become victims of traffickers. According to the US State Department's 2016 *Trafficking in Persons* report, human traffickers have attempted to illegally recruit refugees at reception centers for low-paid work.

In addition to refugees fleeing from conflict, traffickers also target migrant workers who legally enter another country to find work. Migrant workers typically do not speak the nation's language, know few people there, and have limited rights due to their status. As such, they heavily depend on their employers, who can easily exploit them. This is what happened to a woman named Dalisay, who lived in the Philippines. She signed what seemed like a legitimate contract with an employment agency to work as a housemaid in Qatar for $400 a month, in addition to room and board. She hoped to make enough money to send home to her family. Soon after she arrived, however, her employer told her he would only pay her $250 a month. Moreover, she was fed just one meal a day, which consisted of leftovers from the family's lunch. Dalisay was forced to work seven days a week. After she finished cleaning her employer's house, she was forced to clean his mother-in-law's house and then his sister's, without any additional pay.

After eight months, Dalisay attempted to quit, but her boss would not let her leave. Because she was not covered under Qatar's labor laws, Dalisay was subject to *kafala*, Qatar's sponsorship system. Under *kafala* she could not resign, change jobs, leave the country, get a driver's license, or open a checking account without her employer's permission. Her only choice was to run away. Dalisay escaped with fifty-six other women who received shelter at the Philippines Overseas Labor Office.

Life as a Forced Laborer

Until victims can flee or are rescued, their lives are not their own. They have no control over what kind of work they do, how long they work, where they live, whom they can visit, and any other

Young boys in India work in the brick kilns under dire conditions. Families are lured with the promise of decent work, but the circumstances they find constitute forced labor.

aspect of their lives. Everything is completely controlled by their trafficker. For most this means a life of drudgery that often features beatings, starvation, and no medical attention.

An example of this plight comes from the city of Hyderabad, India. Families are lured there with promises of brick-making work, but the circumstances they find constitute forced labor. Their squalid domestic conditions, dangerous working situations, and meager wages are against the law. "They work 12 to 18 hours a day, pregnant women, children, adolescent girls," says Aeshalla Krishna, a labor activist with the human rights group Prayas. "Their diet is poor. There is no good water. They live like slaves."[23] Instead of attending school, children are put to work breaking coal, which is used to heat the clay to make bricks. Men and women stand in water all day, breathing in acrid smoke. The site contractors have been accused of cutting off workers' hands for trying to leave their jobs.

> "They work 12 to 18 hours a day, pregnant women, children, adolescent girls."[23]
>
> —Aeshalla Krishna, human rights activist

The ILO estimates that forced labor victims spend an average of nearly eighteen months in servitude before being rescued or escaping their exploiters. For those who do escape, rebuilding their lives is not an easy process. They are left with many emotional, physical, and economic scars of their experiences.

Victims' Consequences

Being a victim of human trafficking results in major physical, psychological, and even legal consequences. For those who are eventually freed of trafficking, their suffering can continue as they deal with the repercussions of their slavery.

Burned, Beaten, and Starved

Whether a victim of sex or labor trafficking, the physical impacts of the experience are severe and often chronic. For one, victims tend to not get enough to eat during their ordeal. As a result they are malnourished and exhausted. Many also live in unsanitary and crowded living spaces, which increases their chance of getting an infection, virus, or bacterial disease. The combination of poor nutrition and unhygienic living conditions puts victims at risk for a range of health risks and sicknesses, including scabies, tuberculosis, hepatitis, and many other communicable diseases.

At times these conditions can lead to death. In May 2015, for example, the skeletal remains of human trafficking victims were exhumed from mass graves in Malaysia. This is a common trafficking area; as people flee strife in Myanmar and head to Malaysia, they end up victims of human trafficking, usually by agreeing to pay smugglers for their help to cross the border. Once across, if they cannot pay what the smugglers demand, they are forced into either labor or sex work, or both. Many die from the hardships associated with the ordeal. In fact, the remains of at least 139 people were discovered near several human trafficking camps along the Thai-Malaysian border. "They died of poor health, horrible living conditions and illnesses,"[24] says Deputy Inspector-General of Police Noor Rashid Ibrahim.

Many trafficking victims are dehydrated and physically exhausted due to working long hours with little sleep. In Bangladeshi sewing factories, for example, the Institute for Global Labour and Human Rights reports that child victims were sometimes falling down from exhaustion after being forced to work twelve to fourteen hours a day—and sometimes all-night shifts—often seven days a week.

Young garment workers sew clothes on the floor in a factory in Bangladesh. The country's garment industry has been accused of poor factory conditions with little regard for the safety of its workers.

Trafficking victims work in dangerous conditions, too, where little attention is paid to safety. Many work in rooms with poor ventilation or in spaces that have no protection from weather. Workers often lack protective equipment, like hard hats and safety goggles, putting them at higher risk for getting injured or suffering heatstroke or frostbite. According to a 2016 study by Nicola S. Pocock, Ligia Kiss, Sian Oram, and Cathy Zimmerman funded by the Anesvad Foundation and the International Organization for Migration International Development Fund, out of 446 male trafficking victims in Thailand, Cambodia, and Vietnam, almost one-third (29.4 percent) said they had been given no personal protective equipment during their work. Nearly all of those who worked as fishermen (96.7 percent) reported enduring long hours in the open air, often cold or wet from the sea, without a break. The most commonly reported injuries among males were deep cuts and skin injuries; fewer than one-quarter received any medical care. According to Pocock, Kiss, Oram, and Zimmer-

Life as a Beggar

Cambodian Longdy Chhap was just five years old when his family gave him to a broker who promised to take him to Thailand where he could earn money begging. This is how Longdy became one of at least one thousand trafficked child beggars in Thailand. He spent long days sitting on sidewalks and streets asking passersby for money. His trafficker would drop him off at a spot by 5 a.m., then pick him up at 6 p.m. He was warned not to leave his spot for the entire day. If Longdy did not collect enough money, he was not given food. His trafficker kept most of Longdy's earnings, despite promising to send them to his mother.

It was not until Longdy was ten years old that he was finally pulled off the streets by the authorities and placed in a shelter. There, he lashed out, unable to cope with the effects of his experience in a healthy way. "Some staff really hated me because of my behaviour," he says. A counselor helped Longdy adjust to a new life, and as of 2016 he had almost completed a bachelor's degree program in psychology. He also volunteers as a counselor for a local organization that helps children who live in slums. Longdy finally has a new outlook on life and himself. "I don't look down on myself anymore," he says. "I know my background: I was a beggar. But now I'm a counselor."

Quoted in Alisa Tang, "Former Cambodian Child Beggar Triumphs over Trafficked Past to Help Others," Reuters, May 6, 2016. http://in.reuters.com.

man, "Despite the high risk of injury and illness, most reports on migrant and trafficked fishermen note limited or no access to healthcare."[25] Their study found that even those with extreme injuries did not receive care—six victims who worked as fishermen lost body parts, and none received medical care.

Victims also suffer physical violence at the hands of their traffickers. Survivors have reported injuries ranging from bruising and fractures to head trauma. They are routinely beaten or physically punished in other ways. Burns of all types, including deliberate cigarette burns, are a common injury sustained by victims. According to a study of women and adolescents trafficked in Europe, conducted by The London School of Hygiene & Tropical Medicine, more than 70 percent of human trafficking victims interviewed said they experienced physical violence during their victimization.

One such person is Shewaye, an Ethiopian woman who suffered physical abuse as an involuntary domestic servant in Libya. Shewaye worked without pay as a nanny for a relative of former Libyan leader Muammar Gaddhafi. According to the US State Department, Shewaye's trafficker poured scalding hot water over her head and body. She was not allowed to receive medical treatment for her wounds. It was only after a CNN news crew found her that she was freed and able to get treatment.

Sexually Transmitted Diseases and More

Sex trafficking victims suffer a specific set of physical consequences. Victims are particularly susceptible to getting sexually transmitted diseases (STDs), such as gonorrhea, syphilis, urinary tract infections, and pubic lice. They also suffer from pelvic pain, vaginal tearing, rectal trauma, and urinary difficulties. Victims also tend to contract HIV, as evidenced by a 2013 Harvard School of Public Health study. This study analyzed information collected from 1,814 adult female sex workers in Karnataka, India. Researchers found that those who were forced into prostitution (via sex trafficking) were three times more likely to be HIV positive than those who had willingly become sex workers.

Victims of sex trafficking are also likely to experience an unwanted pregnancy due to the nature of their work and the lack

A prostitute with AIDS is comforted by a fellow worker. A Harvard study conducted in India found that those who were forced into prostitution through sex trafficking were three times more likely to be HIV positive than those who willingly chose to become sex workers.

of precautions their traffickers provide for them. Laura Lederer, former senior adviser on *Trafficking in Persons* for the US Department of State, conducted a study of women trafficking victims and found that 55 percent of them had had at least one abortion, and 30 percent had had multiple abortions during the time they were trafficked. More than half indicated that abortion was not their choice, but that their traffickers pressured them into terminating the pregnancy. "I got pregnant six times and had six abortions during this time," said a survivor who participated in the study. "I had severe scar tissue from these abortions, because there was no follow up care. In a couple of cases I had bad infections—so bad that I eventually had to have a hysterectomy [removal of the uterus]."[26] These health problems can have long-term implications and result in a lifetime of chronic pain, infertility, and recurring STD symptoms.

Troubling Psychological Effects

Being a victim of human trafficking also has severe psychological effects, some of which last even longer than the physical effects. Victims suffer so much that they often develop a condition called post-traumatic stress disorder (PTSD), a mental health problem that develops after a person experiences a life-threatening event. Many also become severely depressed and develop substance abuse problems in their attempt to cope. In the worst cases, some commit suicide.

One 2016 study published by Siân Oram of King's College London found that nearly 80 percent of female and 40 percent of male trafficking victims reported high levels of depression, anxiety, and PTSD. "Human trafficking has devastating and long-lasting effects on mental health,"[27] says Oram. A different study of trafficked children, published by the London School of Hygiene & Tropical Medicine in 2015, found that 25 percent have PTSD after being trafficked. Those who suffer from PTSD experience nightmares and flashbacks, are easily startled, have difficulty concentrating and sleeping, and either contemplate or commit suicide.

> "Human trafficking has devastating and long-lasting effects on mental health."[27]
>
> —Siân Oram, professor of Women's Mental Health, King's College London

Margeaux Gray experienced PTSD and other mental health problems as a result of being trafficked. She was sexually abused by a trusted adult who sold her into a child sex-trafficking ring when she was just five years old. The horrific experience produced a lifetime of confusing, conflicting, and difficult emotions for Gray. "I paid a high price," she says. "I've struggled with PTSD, eating disorders and different physical illnesses all related to the trauma of the sexual, physical and psychological abuse."[28]

Victims also view themselves very negatively after surviving a trafficking experience. This is because suffering abuse tends to make people feel worthless, or even like they deserve to be mistreated. According to psychologists, people who live in constant fear often develop feelings of isolation; feel a lack of control over their life; feel helpless and hopeless; and have low self-esteem, self-worth, and self-respect. These feelings can lead people to intentionally hurt themselves, either by cutting themselves, overdosing on

> "I paid a high price. I've struggled with PTSD, eating disorders and different physical illnesses all related to the trauma of the sexual, physical and psychological abuse."[28]
>
> —Margeaux Gray, trafficking victim

drugs, intentionally putting themselves in risky sexual or physical situations, and attempting or committing suicide.

This has been the experience of Jennifer Kempton. Since escaping sex trafficking in 2013, Kempton has dealt with severe emotional trauma. After suffering an abusive childhood, she became a victim of human trafficking when her boyfriend sold her into slavery in Columbus, Ohio. She was held captive for six years, during which time she was raped. She constantly thought of suicide, and even attempted it. Eventually, Kempton managed to escape captivity. Her experiences, however, will haunt her forever. "I suffer from complex PTSD," she explains, as well as "nightmares from the violence inflicted upon me, not to mention the constant struggle of overriding my trust issues."[29] To cope, Kempton founded Survivor's Ink, an organization dedicated to helping victims tattoo over brands or scars left by their captors.

Disrupted Lives

For victims like Kempton, rebuilding a life is not easy. In several countries, victims of sex trafficking are held responsible for the acts they committed while enslaved. In addition, should their slavery be exposed, they are stigmatized or looked down upon by others in society. Consider the case of a nineteen-year-old Vietnamese girl whose father discovered she had been kidnapped by traffickers who forced her to work as a prostitute in China. Her father borrowed money from friends and sold family possessions so he could raise enough to pay the traffickers to release his daughter. Upon her return, however, the girl's father kept the experience secret—he did not report it to the police, nor did he tell any friends or other family members. "I have to keep it quiet," he says. "I cannot tell anyone."[30] He fears that if people knew about his daughter's trauma, she would not be able find a husband or complete her education.

Human trafficking victims also have a lot of trouble reintegrating into normal society. In part this is because they lack the re-

50

sources and ability to live independently. Many people become victims of trafficking because they are poor. After being freed, most return to the same situation but now face the additional hardship of dealing with their traumatic experience. Many own nothing but the clothes on their back; without help, they have no way to get food, shelter, and medical care, let alone psychological care. According to the American Psychological Association, trafficking victims often struggle because they do not have the skills to find housing and jobs, and meet basic needs on their own.

Legal Issues

For some victims the long-term difficulties associated with human trafficking go beyond the physical, psychological, and social; many also have serious legal problems. Sex trafficking victims, particularly those who were forced to work as prostitutes, may end up with a criminal record. In most places, prostitution is illegal, and those caught engaging in it are often charged with criminal

Fear After Escape

Even after they escape, many victims fear that they will be trafficked again, or that their traffickers will find them. This is what Inakoti Venkatalakshmi, of India, fears. She had trouble finding work in her village, so when an agent offered her a lucrative position as a housemaid in Bahrain, she quickly accepted. The agent also offered Venkatalakshmi's oldest daughter work as a housemaid at his house in India.

But once in Bahrain, Venkatalakshmi discovered the salary and working conditions were not what she was promised. "I had to work continuously for at least 18 hours," she recalls. "I felt I would die." Venkatalakshmi ran away, and with the help of Indian social workers in Bahrain, she returned home. However, that was not the end of her ordeal. "The agent in India kept my elder daughter in captivity. She was threatening that she will send my daughter to Bahrain to complete my job contract." With the help of the police, she freed her daughter, but now lives in fear. "As we took police help to rescue my daughter, I am afraid that they will put us in danger," she says. "We don't know where to hide. I don't know any other places where we could go."

Quoted in K. Rejimon, "International Women's Day 2017: Trafficked and Duped, These Women Have Nowhere to Turn," *FirstPost*, March 4, 2017. www.firstpost.com.

Dallas police arrest a young woman for prostitution. Even though sex trafficking victims are forced into prostitution, they can still be arrested for it and end up with a criminal record.

offenses, even if they are victims of trafficking. "I am required to tell prospective employers about prostitution-related charges filed against me between 1980–83," says former victim Beth Jacobs. "In Arizona, I am required to do this for [the rest of my life]. What isn't in my record is the story of a naïve 16-year-old runaway who was 'befriended' by a trafficker, drugged, robbed, beaten, raped, taken to another state and stripped of my identity. For six years, my life as a trafficked sex slave was a daily oppression involving rape and routine beatings."[31] For Jacobs, dealing with a criminal record adds to the harsh fallout of the experience.

People who are trafficked across national borders also face legal issues pertaining to their status. If victims illegally crossed a border, they are at risk of being detained or deported for violating immigration law. To tackle this issue, some countries are making temporary visas (immigration documents that make it legal for noncitizens to stay in a country for a certain amount of time) available to victims if they are willing to testify against their traffickers.

A Lost Childhood

Children who are victims of human trafficking lose something in addition to their physical, mental, and emotional health—a chance at a normal childhood. Instead of attending school, playing with friends, and being on a sports team, their childhood has featured abuse, psychological manipulation, lack of education, separation from family and friends, and inhumane living conditions. It is easy to see why trafficking so greatly impacts a child's emotional, physical, and overall psychological development.

Trafficking impacts children at a key developmental phase in their life. Because they are still growing, the horrors they endure can result in lifelong problems. Rather than being active and well fed, and developing in normal, healthy ways, trafficked children experience constant physical pain and exhaustion. This usually results in physical problems that remain with them long after the experience. "Prolonged abuse in children, including physical and sexual abuse, hunger and malnutrition, may lead to permanent stunting of growth," reports the United Nations Global Initiative to Fight Human Trafficking (UN GIFT). "Trafficked children may suffer, for example, from poorly formed or rotting teeth and may experience reproductive problems at a later date."[32]

> "Prolonged abuse in children, including physical and sexual abuse, hunger and malnutrition, may lead to permanent stunting of growth."[32]
>
> —United Nations Global Initiative to Fight Human Trafficking

Children suffer severe psychological impacts, too. Instead of receiving love and encouragement from family during childhood, trafficked children are often berated and abused, resulting in a constant feeling of fear. This makes them unable to trust others. According to UN GIFT, trafficked children may have great difficulty attaching to family members, teachers, or other adults after their enslavement, as they often find it difficult to trust authority figures. This is exacerbated if it was a family member who sold them to or made a deal with a trafficker. In addition to attachment issues, these children may exhibit antisocial behaviors, aggression, and inappropriate sexual behavior. According to a National Institute of Justice study, being abused or neglected as a child increased a person's likelihood of being arrested as a juvenile by 59 percent. Abuse and neglect also increased the likelihood of adult criminal behavior (by 28 percent) and violent crime (by 30 percent).

If, when returned, children are able to start or return to school, they may struggle due to language, cognitive, and developmental delays and lack memory skills. While other children were attending school, learning and doing homework, trafficked children were performing unspeakable acts in brutal conditions. As a result, both their knowledge and ability to learn are severely impacted, making their return to school difficult. Their problems lead to poor academic performance, and many must repeat grades. Moreover, young victims may find it challenging to adapt to a classroom. They may have trouble interacting with teachers and other students, or struggle to follow the rules. Unless they receive services to overcome these challenges, these students may fail or drop out of school, further decreasing their chances of having an independent and productive future.

Whether old or young, all trafficking victims suffer long after they are rescued or escape from their ordeal. To heal they require assistance to meet their basic needs, get medical care, and address deep-seated psychological issues and emotional pain.

Chapter 5

Fighting Human Trafficking

Focus Questions

1. In what ways is technology being used to fight human trafficking? In what ways do human traffickers use technology to perpetrate their crimes?
2. Should governments provide trafficking victims free medical and psychological services to help them recover from their trauma? Why or why not?
3. Do you believe that using technology to search the Internet for trafficking can violate individuals' privacy? Why or why not?

Nearly two decades ago, the UN passed the Protocol to Prevent, Suppress, and Punish Trafficking in Persons, Especially Women and Children. This piece of legislation helped push human trafficking into the public view. Trafficking had long been an issue that had been swept aside, or even ignored, by the international community—the UN Protocol helped change that. It resulted in countries putting more effort into recognizing and combating human trafficking through awareness, laws, and law enforcement. According to Anne T. Gallagher, a legal adviser who works with the Australia-Asia Trafficking in Persons Program, "The Trafficking Protocol proved to be a game-changer, triggering unprecedented levels of action."[33] The protocol entered into force on December 25, 2003, and as of mid-2017, 170 countries—including the United States—had adopted it.

As a result, more countries have strengthened their public awareness programs regarding human trafficking. They have also taken steps to provide training and resources so that law enforcement has more tools with which to combat the problem. Likewise, they have added and strengthened laws regarding human trafficking. A main result of the protocol is that more countries now criminalize trafficking than ever before: just 33 regarded it as an illegal, prosecutable act in 2003, but by August 2016, 158 had done so. Once a country agrees to the protocol, its government is supposed to implement laws that criminalize trafficking, but not all have followed through.

The 3P Approach

The UN and member countries fight human trafficking using an approach known as 3P, which stands for prevention, protection, and prosecution. This approach articulates specific requirements for preventing human trafficking, prosecuting traffickers, and protecting victims.

Prevention, the first P, refers to conducting public awareness and education campaigns about the signs of human trafficking so it can be reported. It also includes amending labor laws so they protect all workers, including migrants, from unfair practices, such as refusing to pay wages or holding on to workers' identification documents, such as passports. Another aspect of prevention involves enforcing labor laws and developing and monitoring labor recruitment programs to protect workers from being exploited.

The second P stands for protection, and this is the most victim-centric aspect of the approach. Countries focused on protection implement measures to provide for victims' physical, psychological, and social recovery. The final P stands for prosecution, which includes establishing laws that make human trafficking illegal and prosecuting those who break them. The goal of such laws is to deter trafficking by demonstrating authorities' ability and will to convict traffickers.

Overall, the 3P approach has resulted in more global prosecutions, more reporting of trafficking (by both victims and witnesses), and more assistance for victims. According to the UNODC's *Global Report on Trafficking in Persons, 2016*, since the Protocol was ratified, the number of countries that criminalize trafficking has increased fivefold. For example, the government of the Philippines established anti-trafficking laws according to the 3P approach in 2003 and 2012. These laws provided more funding to

The United Nations and member countries' fight against human trafficking emphasizes public awareness and education campaigns. Pictured is a Thai government campaign poster at the international airport in Bangkok, a city with one of the highest incidences of sex trafficking in the world.

STOP HUMAN TRAFFICKING ☎1300

YOU MAKE YOUR CHOICES.

train and hire law enforcement, among other things. As a result, 595 traffickers were prosecuted in 2014, and more than 569 were prosecuted in 2015.

Elsewhere, increased awareness campaigns have led to greater reports of trafficking. In 2016, for example, the anti-trafficking organization Polaris reported an increase in calls and texts to its trafficking hotline that led to the initiation of eight thousand trafficking cases (up from 5,961 cases in 2015).

Additionally, more countries around the world are providing services to victims. For example, Myanmar recently opened a shelter for human trafficking victims along the Thailand-Myanmar border where trafficking is prevalent. It has also increased training of its public officials on how to assist victims.

The United States: What Works to Curb Trafficking

The United States has made the issue of human trafficking a core concern of its foreign and domestic policy. Since the late nineties, Congress has passed eleven laws to address the issue, and has increasingly strengthened them. In 2000 Congress approved the Trafficking Victims Protection Act, which created the first comprehensive federal law to address trafficking. It also established human trafficking and related offenses as federal crimes, and gave them severe penalties.

Since then, the government has passed more trafficking-related laws, such as one that states that sex trafficking prosecutions involving children do not require proof of the use of force, fraud, or coercion. This means that any youth under eighteen involved in sex trafficking is considered a victim, even if he or she has consented. Another law, passed in 2013, prohibits the use of fraud to recruit workers for work performed in the United States

Survivors of human trafficking participate in a congressional briefing to discuss solutions to prevent human trafficking. They provide valuable insights for law enforcement and policy makers.

or elsewhere on a US government contract. In addition, in 2015, the United States passed a law that allows survivors to have formal input into federal anti-trafficking policy. Survivors have valuable insights into the effects of trafficking raids on victims and why some victims decline assistance, and law enforcement and politicians benefit from their knowledge when determining policies and procedures.

To further understand human trafficking, its perpetrators, and its victims, in 2015 the US Advisory Council on Human Trafficking was created; it is composed of eleven survivors of human trafficking who help analyze trafficking cases. "The fact that survivors are engaging with the federal government on this level is truly amazing,"[34] asserts council cochair Sheila White, who was forced into sex work as a child. Efforts like this have helped federal law enforcement agencies secure four thousand convictions against traffickers and identify more than two thousand victims of human trafficking since 2008.

> "The fact that survivors are engaging with the federal government on this level is truly amazing."[34]
>
> —Sheila White, cochair of the US Advisory Council on Human Trafficking

Prevention Methods

A key way to fight trafficking is to prevent it before it occurs. Prevention methods focus on teaching people how to recognize a potential trafficking situation, what to do if someone suspects he or she is being trafficked, and how to respond in the event someone witnesses trafficking. Because prevention is so critical, it underscores the goals of public awareness campaigns like those conducted by Polaris.

Polaris's public awareness campaign features billboards, cards, commercials, and posters that advertise a twenty-four-hour National Human Trafficking Resource Center that provides human trafficking victims and survivors a way to report trafficking and get access to support and services. The center has a hotline number, an e-mail address, and a mobile phone number that allows victims, survivors, and witnesses to reach it at all hours. Thousands of suspected human trafficking cases have been reported to the center via e-mail, phone, and text. In fact, from

2016 to 2017, Polaris responded to over twenty-five thousand calls, texts, and e-mails that ranged from service assistance requests from victims to tips about suspected trafficking.

Governments and nongovernmental organizations (NGOs) have also developed prevention methods that are specifically tailored to victims. In many regions, poverty is a key risk factor for being trafficked. Given this, prevention efforts aim to provide services such as education and health care that offer potential victims the stability they need to avoid becoming trafficked. One NGO in Vietnam uses this method. It operates in remote areas populated by ethnic minorities who are at high risk for trafficking. It helped legally register about two thousand residents, which allowed them to access government benefits such as health care, financial assistance, and education. People who live in remote locations tend to not be aware of these benefits or how to obtain these services. By registering and receiving services, people are better able to meet their basic needs, which makes them less likely to become vulnerable to human trafficking.

Focus on Technology

Other countries are using technology to find traffickers and rescue victims. Traffickers have long used social media, websites, and apps to recruit victims using deceptive and coercive methods, and to advertise to potential buyers. Now law enforcement agencies are using the same technology to pursue the traffickers.

In 2015 the US Defense Advanced Research Projects Agency (DARPA) started the Memex program. This is a partnership of groups from various universities and companies that creates online tools that collect content that is usually ignored by or unavailable to commercial search engines. The teams then analyze the content for hidden patterns and build models to predict behavior. Authorities use Memex to search the Internet for anything related to human trafficking, such as advertisements used to lure victims into servitude or materials that promote their sexual exploitation. This content tends to exist in something called the "deep Web," which Google, Yahoo, and other popular search engines do not index. Memex is able to find and track these ads, and officials use its results to find leads and build cases against traffickers. To date, Memex has discovered more than 100 million escort (pros-

Backpage.com

Backpage.com is a classified advertising website, somewhat like Craigslist. It offers a variety of products and services, including car ads, jobs listings, real estate posts—and advertisements for adult services. In 2011 Backpage's adult services subsection was accused of serving as a vehicle for sex trafficking, particularly of youth.

Kubiiki Pride found this out in a shocking way. Pride was scrolling through ads on Backpage when she saw an advertisement for her fourteen-year-old daughter, who had been missing for nine months. In the photo, Pride could see that her daughter was only partially dressed. Pride notified police, but did not want to wait for them to act, so she posed as a customer and "ordered" her own daughter from the ad. By doing this, Pride was reunited with her daughter, who had cigarette burns on 80 percent of her body.

Because of stories like Pride's, the US government has investigated Backpage. As a result Backpage suspended sexual advertising on its site, the company's CEO was the focus of a 2017 Senate investigation, and parents of trafficked children advertised on its site are now seeking legal restitution. According to Pride, "For years, I tried to tell everyone that would listen about the crimes Backpage was committing, but now more of the government is becoming aware and I am hopeful a change is coming."

Quoted in Millicent Smith, "Mother Finds Missing Teenage Daughter Being Sold on Website, Fights Back," *Chattanooga (TN) Times Free Press*, February 24, 2017. www.timesfreepress.com.

titution) advertisements and uncovered patterns that have helped agents zero in on organized trafficking rings.

DARPA also funds Bashpole Software, Inc., a firm that develops technology called idTraffickers, which helps locate victims of human trafficking. idTraffickers uses biometric technology (including facial recognition) to compare images of missing persons against images from human trafficking databases and online escort ads. Law enforcement agencies use the software to identify victims and track criminals. Citizens can use it too; if people see someone they think may be involved in human trafficking, they can take their picture and text it to a number provided by Bashpole, which will then use idTraffickers to search the Internet and forward reports of matches to law enforcement agencies.

Microsoft's PhotoDNA is another technology that identifies images. However, instead of biometrics, it assigns hash values, or numbers, to tiny grids of an image to give it a specific identification, or "PhotoDNA." The National Center for Missing & Exploited Children (NCMEC) uses PhotoDNA to analyze known images of child pornography and assign them an ID. The NCMEC then shares this information with online service providers, which search the Internet for pictures that have the same ID information (this works because such images are often uploaded and shared many times). The NCMEC can use the matches to stop the images from being distributed and potentially locate the people who are distributing them.

Online services such as Facebook also use PhotoDNA to find child pornography on its site, and to block images from being

The online service giant Facebook uses special programs that help it identify and block child pornography on its site. It also reports any incidents to law enforcement agencies so they can conduct investigations.

uploaded. PhotoDNA alerts Facebook if someone attempts to upload what appears to be child pornography. Facebook then reports the incident to the NCMEC, which begins an initial investigation and contacts local law enforcement officers. Law enforcement agencies say these techniques have had a significant effect on their ability to fight child sex trafficking and exploitation. "It's basically made things easier, so that we can find people who are sharing child porn on the Internet," San Jose police sergeant Greg Lombardo says of the technology. "They can just have a computer running all the time, searching."[35]

Protecting the Victims

Fighting human trafficking also involves helping victims after they have escaped or been rescued. This is critical not just to helping them rebuild their lives, but for preventing them from being re-trafficked. To this end, the US Department of Health and Human Services (HHS) funds the National Human Trafficking Resource Center, which runs a hotline for trafficking victims, law enforcement officers, and victim advocates. Callers are given information about a range of services available to them, from shelters and legal services to a national database of organizations and individuals who work in the anti-trafficking field. In 2015 HHS awarded grants that helped 183 agencies to provide legal, medical, employment, and education services to victims. According-ing to Loretta Lynch, the former US attorney general, "In our nation's fight against human trafficking, it is not enough to bring perpetrators to justice; we must also ensure that survivors can access the resources they need to rebuild their lives and reclaim their futures."[36]

> "[PhotoDNA] basically made things easier, so that we can find people who are sharing child porn on the Internet."[35]
>
> —Greg Lombardo, San Jose police sergeant

It is expensive to help victims, and countries with fewer resources have more trouble doing so. For this reason, the UN Voluntary Trust Fund has committed money to a variety of global organizations that help victims of human trafficking. In 2015 this fund distributed grants to nineteen new projects that provide

Hotel Warnings

As a child, Anneke Lucas suffered through five-and-a-half years of being tortured and raped at the hands of human traffickers. These horrors most often took place in hotels. This is why today, Lucas is a passionate advocate for passing laws that would require hotels to put up notices that explain the signs of human trafficking and list contact information for the National Human Trafficking Resource Center Hotline. Such laws would also require hotel staff to receive training on how to spot victims.

Lucas believes such legislation would accomplish three things: 1) it would help hotels and hotel guests spot signs of human trafficking; 2) it could give victims the courage to report the crime; and 3) it would discourage traffickers from using hotels to conduct illegal activity. Such legislation has already passed in Connecticut, and Lucas has created an online petition to pass a similar law in New York. "I was the kind of child that wanted to get help but there was none," Lucas told NBC News.

Quoted in Kalhan Rosenblatt, "Human Trafficking in Hotels: New York Lawmaker Teams Up with Advocate," NBC News, March 21, 2017. www.nbcnews.com.

direct assistance to victims. One NGO, Dhaka Ahsania Mission, in Bangladesh, received funding to provide shelters to protect, rehabilitate, and reintegrate human trafficking victims. While at the shelter, victims have their basic needs met (food, beds, and medical care). Victims also receive job training and placement and can take advantage of legal help to file cases against their traffickers.

However, victims ultimately need much more to successfully reintegrate into society. Young victims need special assistance to ensure they are not re-trafficked. One place doing this is the Avanti House in Colorado. There, formerly trafficked victims can receive specialized therapeutic foster care specifically designed for girls who have been sex trafficked. The girls are taught life skills, receive on-site medical care, and have access to psychological treatment and education. "Once we know a girl is long-term, we have milestones that we'll be working on," says Kristen Harness, the executive director of Avanti House. "Within 60–90 days, we want her to be actively involved in school. These girls are at least one to two years behind."[37] Harness's goal is to provide special services to as many sex trafficking victims in Colorado as her group home is allowed to accommodate by the state.

Looking to the Future

Despite these efforts, the fight against human trafficking remains very challenging. Countries must grapple with finding ways to help victims, prosecute traffickers, and prevent the industry from thriving in the first place. Progress is impeded by multiple challenges, including varying levels of effort and funding. In addition the world's wide variety of cultures, economies, and religions affect how countries view and implement human trafficking laws. While more countries have laws against trafficking than ever before, the average number of convictions remains low.

Fighting trafficking is a complicated endeavor. Somaly Mam knows this well, as she is a survivor of sexual slavery and a human rights leader who has spent more than two decades fighting this issue. Mam thinks the fight against human trafficking works best when it includes prosecuting traffickers, empowering victims, and addressing the root causes of slavery. "To many people, the issue of slavery seems like a clear case of right and wrong," writes Mam. "The reality is much more complicated. There are many root causes and serious challenges. But these challenges do not stop me from continuing to find solutions to eradicate slavery and empower its survivors as part of the solution."[38]

> "To many people, the issue of slavery seems like a clear case of right and wrong. The reality is much more complicated. There are many root causes and serious challenges."[38]
>
> —Somaly Mam, sex trafficking survivor and human rights leader

Source Notes

Introduction: Modern-Day Slavery

1. Somaly Mam, "How to End Modern Slavery and Human Trafficking," *Forbes*, November 11, 2015. www.forbes.com.
2. Quoted in Siddharth Kara, "A $110 Loan, Then 20 Years of Debt Bondage," The CNN Freedom Project, June 2, 2011. http://thecnnfreedomproject.blogs.cnn.com.
3. Quoted in Amanda Milkovits, "Fighting for Her Soul: A Sex Trafficking Victim's Story," *Providence Journal*, November 15, 2014. www.providencejournal.com.

Chapter 1: Understanding Human Trafficking

4. United Nations, "The Universal Declaration of Human Rights," December 10, 1948. www.un.org.
5. Quoted in UN News Centre, "Global Treaties Provide Blueprint to 'Seal Cracks' in Legal Regime on Human Trafficking—UN Anti-Crime Chief," October 16, 2007. www.un.org.
6. Quoted in Ruth Evans, "Pakistani Police Rescue 24 from Organ Trafficking Gang," BBC, January 24, 2017. www.bbc.com.
7. Quoted in the Office of the Secretary-General's Envoy on Youth, "Child Marriages: 39,000 Every Day—More than 140 Million Girls Will Marry Between 2011 and 2020," March 7, 2013. www.un.org/youthenvoy.
8. UNODC, *Global Report on Trafficking in Persons, 2016*, United Nations. www.unodc.org.
9. Polaris, "The Victims & Traffickers," 2017. https://polarisproject.org.

Chapter 2: Sex Trafficking

10. Quoted in Rafael Romo, "Human Trafficking Survivor: I Was Raped 43,200 Times," CNN, November 10, 2015. www.cnn.com.

11. Michelle Lille, "The Connection Between Sex Trafficking and Pornography," Human Trafficking Search, April 14, 2014. www.humantraffickingsearch.net.
12. Quoted in Edgar Walters, Neena Satija, and Morgan Smith, "Sold Out: Imprisoned Pimps Tell How They Recruit, Sell Girls," *Waco (TX) Tribune-Herald*, February 13, 2017. www.wacotrib.com.
13. Amanda Walker-Rodriguez and Rodney Hill, "Human Sex Trafficking," *FBI Law Enforcement Bulletin*, March 2011. https://leb.fbi.gov.
14. Quoted in Habiba Nosheen and Anup Kaphle, "For Nepali Girls Trafficked to Indian Brothels, Where Is Home?," *Atlantic,* November 30, 2011. www.theatlantic.com.
15. Quoted in Adriana Hauser and Mariano Castillo, "A Heavy Toll for the Victims of Human Trafficking," CNN, April 26, 2013. www.cnn.com.
16. Quoted in Danielle Chemtob, "Isolation. Fear. Manipulation. Marin's Hidden Trafficking Industry," Redwood H.S. *Bark*, April 2015. http://redwoodbark.org.
17. Heather M. Smith, "Sex Trafficking: Trends, Challenges, and the Limitations of International Law," Lewis & Clark College, November 19, 2010. http://college.lclark.edu/live/files/10777.

Chapter 3: Forced Labor

18. Quoted in End Slavery Now, "Flor Molina," January 1, 2015. www.endslaverynow.org.
19. Quoted in Anti-Slavery International, "India: Debt Bondage," 2017. www.antislavery.org.
20. Quoted in Dana Ford, "Jury Convicts Georgia Woman of Trafficking 2 Nigerian Women," CNN, July 13, 2011. www.cnn.com.
21. Quoted in Robyn Dixon, "Slavery Still Haunts Africa, Where Millions Remain Captive," *LA Times*, October 17, 2013. http://articles.latimes.com.
22. Quoted in Mansur Mirovalev and Andrew Kramer, "In Uzbekistan, the Practice of Forced Labor Lives On During the Cotton Harvest," *New York Times,* December 17, 2013. www.nytimes.com.
23. Quoted in Humphrey Hawksley, "Why India's Brick Kiln Workers 'Live like Slaves,'" BBC, January 2, 2014. www.bbc.com.

Chapter 4: Victims' Consequences

24. Quoted in Jonathan Edward, "Malnutrition Cause of Death in Malaysia-Thai Trafficking Route Victims, Autopsy Shows," *Malay Mail Online*, April 15, 2016. www.themalaymailonline.com.

25. Nicola S. Pocock, Ligia Kiss, Sian Oram, and Cathy Zimmerman, "Labour Trafficking Among Men and Boys in the Greater Mekong Subregion: Exploitation, Violence, Occupational Health Risks, and Injuries," *PLOS One*, December 16, 2016. http://journals.plos.org.

26. Quoted in Genevieve Plaster, "Shock Study: 55% of Sex-Trafficking Victims Become Pregnant, Forced into Abortions," LifeNews, September 14, 2014. www.lifenews.com.

27. Quoted in Joshua A. Krisch, "The Psychology of a Human Trafficking Victim," Vocativ, April 15, 2016. www.vocativ.com.

28. Quoted in Beth Smith, "Human Trafficking Survivor Speaks Out," *Evansville (IN) Courier & Press*, December 31, 2014. www.courierpress.com.

29. Quoted in Alex Davessar, "Human Trafficking: A Survivor's Story," The Pioneer (Cuyahoga Falls, OH), November 15, 2016. http://thepioneerwjhs.com.

30. Quoted in Phillip Martin, "Underground Trade: Part Six," *Huffington Post*, March 4, 2013. www.huffingtonpost.com.

31. Beth Jacobs, "Former Sex Slave: Arizona Can Do More to Stop Abuse," AZCentral, January 22, 2104. www.azcentral.com.

32. United Nations Global Initiative to Fight Human Trafficking, *An Introduction to Human Trafficking: Vulnerability, Impact, and Action*, UNODC, 2008. www.unodc.org.

Chapter 5: Fighting Human Trafficking

33. Anne T. Gallagher, "Two Cheers for the Trafficking Protocol," *Anti-Trafficking Review,* 2015. www.antitraffickingreview.org.

34. Quoted in Steve Herman, "Victims of Modern Slave Trade Call for Better Law Enforcement Training," VOA News, October 18, 2016. www.voanews.com.

35. Quoted in Mike Cassidy, "Facebook Is Part of a High Tech Posse Fighting Child Pornography," *San Jose (CA) Mercury News*, January 11, 2013. www.mercurynews.com.

36. Quoted in US Department of Justice, "Civil Legal Aid Supports Federal Efforts to Help Human Trafficking Victims," Legal Aid Interagency Roundtable (LAIR), February 2016. www.justice.gov/lair.

37. Quoted in Brittany Werges, "For the First Time, Denver's Underage Victims of Sex Trafficking Have a Place to Call Their Own," *303 Magazine*, February 9, 2017. https://303magazine.com.

38. Mam, "How to End Modern Slavery and Human Trafficking."

How to Get Involved

By getting involved, you can make a difference. Organizations that work to stop human trafficking often need volunteers for a variety of tasks ranging from letter-writing to organizing events. Some organizations also sponsor internships for youth.

Coalition to Abolish Slavery & Trafficking (CAST)

5042 Wilshire Blvd. #586
Los Angeles, CA 90036
website: www.castla.org

CAST provides services to survivors of human trafficking and partners with over one hundred cultural and faith-based community groups to fight trafficking. CAST also advocates anti-trafficking legislation. Individuals can volunteer by e-mailing and faxing letters regarding wanted legislation, which is listed on its website, to representatives.

Free the Slaves

320 Nineteenth St. NW, Suite 600
Washington, DC 20036
website: www.freetheslaves.net

The mission of Free the Slaves is to help people escape slavery, prevent others from becoming trapped, and bring slaveholders to justice. Individuals can assist the organization by downloading their online materials to teach others about the issue and learn which companies use slavery-free products and which do not.

Hope for Justice

PO Box 50165
Nashville, TN 37205
website: hopeforjustice.org

Hope for Justice aims to end human trafficking by rescuing its victims and reforming legislation. Individuals can assist its mission by hosting fund-raisers benefiting the nonprofit organization, sharing awareness images provided by the organization on social media, and learning to spot the signs of human trafficking and how to report it.

International Justice Mission (IJM)
PO Box 58147
Washington, DC 20037
website: www.ijm.org

The goal of IJM is to protect the most vulnerable people from violence, including human trafficking, in the developing world by assisting law enforcement with rescuing victims. IJM has seventeen field offices in Africa, Latin America, South Asia, and Southeast Asia. Individuals can help by signing a petition on its website and sharing it with others.

Polaris
PO Box 65323
Washington, DC 20035
website: https://polarisproject.org

This nonprofit organization helps survivors restore their freedom, prevents the abuse of more victims, and uses data and technology to pursue traffickers. On its website are petitions for legislation to protect victims and pursue traffickers; individuals can sign them, share them with others, and e-mail them to their legislators.

UNICEF
125 Maiden Ln.
New York, NY 10038
website: www.unicefusa.org

UNICEF's mission is to save and protect the world's most vulnerable children, and one aspect of this goal is the fight against child trafficking. On its website are ways individuals can assist the organization, such as signing the online pledge, starting a UNICEF club at school, and educating themselves and others to buy products that are not the result of child labor.

For Further Research

Books

Alexis A. Aronowitz, *Human Trafficking: A Reference Handbook*. Santa Barbara, CA: ABC-CLIO, 2017.

Kevin Bales and Ron Soodalter, *The Slave Next Door: Human Trafficking and Slavery in America Today.* Berkeley: University of California Press, 2010.

Nita Belles, *In Our Backyard: Human Trafficking in America and What We Can Do to Stop It.* Grand Rapids, MI: BakerBooks, 2015.

Stephanie Hepburn, *Human Trafficking Around the World: Hidden in Plain Sight.* New York: Columbia University Press, 2013.

Jenni S. Jessen, *The Lucky One: A Chilling True Account of Child Sex Trafficking and One Survivor's Journey from Brutal Captivity to a Life of Freedom*. Colorado Springs, CO: Compass 31, 2016.

Katariina Rosenblatt, with Cecil Murphey, *Stolen: The True Story of a Sex Trafficking Survivor*. Grand Rapids, MI: Revell, 2014.

Louise Shelley, *Human Trafficking: A Global Perspective.* New York: Cambridge University Press, 2010.

Internet Sources

Leif Coorlim and Dana Ford, "Sex Trafficking: The New American Slavery," CNN, March 14, 2017. www.cnn.com/2015/07/20/us /sex-trafficking.

Jessica Heslam, "Special Report: Opiate Crisis Pushes Addicts to Sex Trade," *Boston Herald,* March 13, 2017. www.boston herald.com/news/local_coverage/2017/03/special_report _opiate_crisis_pushes_addicts_to_sex_trade.

Sebastien Malo, "Nearly 500 Arrested in California Human Trafficking Raids," Reuters, February 1, 2017. www.reuters.com /article/us-usa-trafficking-arrests-idUSKBN15G5J6.

Heather Poole, "What Being a Flight Attendant Taught Me About Human Trafficking," Mashable, January 12, 2016. http://mash able.com/2016/01/12/how-to-spot-human-trafficking/#Y5EwB Um67Pqi.

Marty Stempniak, "Human Trafficking: How America's Hospitals Can Help," H&HN, March 21, 2017. www.hhnmag.com /articles/8159-human-trafficking-how-americas-hospitals-can -help.

Timothy Williams, "Backpage's Sex Ads Are Gone. Child Trafficking, Hardly," *New York Times*, March 11, 2017. www.nytimes .com/2017/03/11/us/backpage-ads-sex-trafficking.html.

Index

Picture Credits

Cover: iStockphoto/chameleonseye

7: Associated Press

11: Osugi/Shutterstock.com

15: Evelyn Hockstein/KRT/Newscom

20: kuzmafoto/Shutterstock.com

24: Yui Mok/ZUMA Press/Newscom

26: Shutterstock.com

29: Associated Press

35: Associated Press

39: Maximum Exposure PR/Shutterstock.com

42: Sushavan Nandy/ZUMA Press/Newscom

45: Associated Press

48: Karl Grobl/ZUMA Press/Newscom

52: Associated Press

57: Barbara Walton/EPA/Newscom

58: Associated Press

62: Rawpixel.com/Shutterstock.com

About the Author

Leanne K. Currie-McGhee has been an education writer for over a decade. She lives in Norfolk, Virginia, with her husband, Keith, daughters Hope and Grace, and dog, Delilah.

Eager Street Academy #884
401 East Eager Street
Baltimore, MD 21202

BOOK CHARGING CARD

Accession No. _____ Call No. _____

Author_____

Title _____

Date Loaned	Borrower's Name	Date Ret...